MASTER TIME IN 10 MINUTES A DAY

TIME MANAGEMENT TIPS FOR ANYONE STRUGGLING WITH WORK – LIFE BALANCE

BY MICHAL STAWICKI

www.michalzone.com

September 2014
Copyright © 2014 Michal Stawicki
All rights reserved worldwide.
ISBN: 1500187739
ISBN-13: 978-1500187736

Table of Contents

4

1

Introduction

"Time is what we want most, but what we use worst."

- William Penn

I won't bore you to death by preaching about the importance of time management, about how time is your most precious commodity and cannot be bought or reclaimed, about how we all have the same amount of it, or how the thing setting us apart is how we make use of it and *blah, blah, blah*. Enough has already been written about that, by visionaries and eggheads alike. I do not need to reaffirm the importance of your own life, your own time. Chances are, if you are reading this book, your life and time are already of great value to you.

Whatever your goal may be, I assume you are not in the position to drop everything else and commit all your resources - especially your time - to fulfilling it. Your life is an ongoing project, not something to make from scratch starting today.

Theoretical ruminations have their place, but this book will not be one. Since you are committing some of your valuable time to read this book, you likely have some questions: does the author of this book know more about time management than I do? How effectively does he use his time? Is he a person I can follow? Is his advice applicable in my situation? These are good questions to be asking; they show that you put energy into determining if something is worth your time. Well, fear not

I think you can relate to me. I'm what you might consider an ordinary person, not an ivory tower guru. I commute, work a 9 to 5 job, have a family and attend church regularly.

As far as my qualifications go, I will leave you to draw your own conclusions. I don't know you and what you can squeeze into 24 hours, but have a look at my typical day and compare it to your own:

I'm a full time employee and my total daily commute adds about three and half hours to each workday.

I know the importance of sleep to one's overall state of being, so I try very hard to sleep at least seven hours a day (which usually means I get six and a half).

Every day for me also includes 20 minutes of prayer, 60-90 minutes of writing and at least 30 minutes of reading.

Additionally, I spend about 15 minutes on meditation and self-analysis every morning.

I exercise 20 to 30 minutes per day and listen to educational and/or motivational materials for 20 minutes.

Every day, I review my 1,300-word personal mission statement. I study the Bible, read professional literature and practice speed reading, each for about 10 minutes per day.

I keep three different gratitude journals - one about my wife, one about my kids and one about my life as a whole. I have a very personal blog, (another journal, really) and I post there daily, taking another 5-10 minutes.

I'm involved in a few online communities on a daily basis, and I learn about writing, publishing and marketing by following a few blogs.

If you have been doing the mental math, you've seen that my daily commitments (sleep included) add up to at least 23 hours of each day. Yes, I do still find time to breathe. To track my progress and dedication to my daily tasks, check me out on Lift, https://www.lift.do/users/360e9cc8df81879e1935

Many people set goals to build new habits, but then abandon them too quickly. The power of daily habits, if sustained, is immense. I've written about 150,000 words in 2013 - just for my blogs, short stories and books. I've read more than 40 books and hundreds of blog posts. I have a whole notepad full of the self-knowledge I've gained - my goals, plans, desires, motivations, obstacles, dreams, doubts and beliefs.

In addition to the tasks I complete every day, I also have other weekly, monthly and irregular commitments. For more than 16 years, I have been an active member of my church community. This adds three to five hours of commitments weekly. Additionally, every month I take the time to make a financial statement for the past month and budget estimation for the next.

You might think, with all of those regular commitments, I would be tapped out at the end of each day. But, as you will see, my productivity doesn't end there. In addition to all my daily tasks, I've launched 3 WordPress sites since the beginning of 2013 - a personal blog, a blog for me as an author, and also a project that's a little harder to define - www.onedollartips.com. I manage all three sites on my own. First, I had to learn how to create and manage WordPress sites. Then it was off to learn how to buy a domain and hosting, how to merge different domains onto one hosting platform, how to remove spam comments, how to install and manage plugins, updates and widgets. I had to discover how to make sense of my website analytics. And the list goes on.

I've made a lot of personal development materials for my own use. I've recorded several hours of audio and rewritten the book, *The Science of Getting Rich,* in its entirety to make it more congruent with my faith and values.

I overcame my shyness. I talk with strangers from time to time and always send a smile their way.

I also published five Kindle books in 2013. That process involves so much more than just writing -

research, cover design, formatting, marketing, payment, and tax issues. And, the list goes on.

I have a couple of other projects which haven't seen the sunlight yet.

I've even found time to devote to my hobbies; in August 2013, I organized and participated in a collectable card game tournament.

Last, but certainly not least, I've been married since 2000 and I have three kids. My family is important to me and I give them as much of my time and attention as I can: dates with my wife, games with my kids, reading to my daughter, doing homework with my boys. Walks, chats, going to the circus, cinema, theatre or swimming pool.

I also found time to take a two-week vacation. While on vacation, I took a complete break from working and writing. It was enjoyable and refreshing.

I didn't share this background with you just to impress you. I wrote all of this because I imagine that you can relate. Take a moment to compare your story with mine. If it sounds similar and you want to learn my productivity concepts, then this book is for you.

If you have more obligations and projects, if you find that you are already more productive, reading this book might not be an effective use of your time. My goal is to serve you, not disadvantage you, so if that's the case - skip this book.

I want to show you how to extract more value from your time and find more fulfilment in your life. So, if you are now curious how I do all this and reconcile it with a full time job - read on.

This book has recently gotten a few negative comments with one common theme: *"Nothing new here."* All I have to say in reply is: This is a book about mastering your time, not about fashion. If you're looking for novelty, look somewhere else!

Action Items

Read the introduction and make four lists (actually write these down):

- Daily Obligations
- Weekly Obligations
- Monthly and Irregular Obligations
- Goals

Compare our lists and see if your time constraints and aspirations look similar to mine.

If you feel you stand to benefit by reading my methods to time management, read on!

2

The 10 Minute Philosophy

"The future is something which everyone reaches at the rate of 60 minutes an hour, whatever he does, whoever he is."

— C.S. Lewis

Entrepreneur and motivational speaker Jim Rohn was convinced that **true life changes are driven by one's personal philosophy**. He perceived his whole life's journey as nothing more than an outcome of his attitudes and beliefs. When he was young, Jim blamed other people and external factors for his failures, and his life was a mess. When he changed his way of thinking, when he took accountability for creating his own success, he found himself happy and with money in the bank. In fact, these things began changing immediately.

I share this example because this belief is a cornerstone of my philosophy.

Managing your time is a lifelong commitment. As long as you live, you will always have time to manage. It is one of a very few commodities we all have in common. *"The time will pass anyway; we might just as well put that passing time to the best possible use."* Earl Nightingale said brilliantly.

Mastering the art of time management requires patience, perseverance and commitment. As Jim Rohn's story shows, these traits must come from within. You need a solid personal philosophy to distill such qualities within yourself. I have such a philosophy which allows me to wake up every day with enthusiasm and determination, and I know it can work for you too. From my experience:

I KNOW that daily, sustained action brings results.

I know this because I practice this rule in every area of my life. I focus daily on specific actions, committing 10 minutes to them. I track my results, and I see them blossom. I see the results every day in such diverse areas as physical fitness, finances, learning and relationships. I believe that this is a universal law, applicable to absolutely **every** aspect of life.

The more action taken, the better the results ... up to a point. Take a look at the chart below.

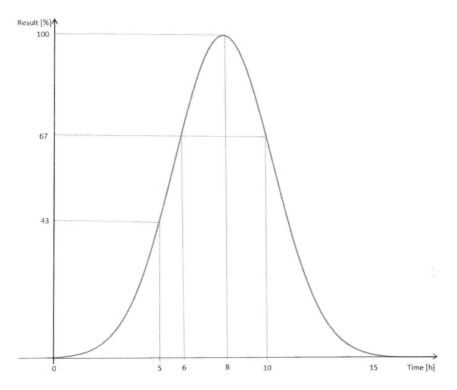

The shape of the curve above is called normal distribution in probability research. In statistics, it is an almost universal truth, much like the number π is in math. As π can be found in many equations describing the texture of the universe, normal distribution can be used to describe a multitude of measures in our world including a person's IQ, height or weight to name a few. According to the Central Limit Theorem, the average of a large number of random variables tends toward normal distribution. In our big and complicated world, nearly everything can represented by a huge amount of data. If you want to know more about the CLT in depth, check out this easy-to-understand presentation: http://askville.amazon.com/Central-

Limit-Theorem-apply-statistics-
life/AnswerViewer.do?requestId=7620607

I believe normal distribution can be also applied to describe the relationship between effort (which consumes time), and achieved results. Even the smallest amount of invested time brings results. I consciously use a few minutes of my day on financial planning. Those monthly finance tasks I take on - a budget summary, bill-paying, dividing my resources between different assets and so on - take me about two hours per month, which works out to roughly four minutes a day. Breaking it down to a daily task has driven incredible results; I save almost five times more money than I did a year ago!

As you will also note, however, the shape of the normal distribution reaches a point where it peaks and then begins decreasing. This speaks to another truth: the Law of Diminishing Returns. The Law of Diminishing Returns tells us that more is better … to a certain point. Let's say that you are a car nut and have always wanted to own a Ferrari. So you work hard, save, and finally are able to buy a Ferrari. You would probably get great pleasure from owning your shiny, red Ferrari, from driving it, seeing it in your garage, and from going to rallies with other Ferrari owners. Now let's say that you got hooked and kept buying Ferraris until you owned 20 of them. At that point, it is likely that the amount of joy you felt in buying your 20th Ferrari would not be nearly as great as you felt buying the first or second Ferrari.

Effort, it seems, follows the same law. For every activity there is a "sweet spot" of effort, a point at which you extract the most value from the time spent. Every activity or goal will have a different point at which this occurs and it will take some experimentation to determine where that "sweet spot" is for you, for each of your tasks. There are a few explanations for this. In some cases, the point of maximum returns occurs when you reach peak efficiency or when you complete a task thoroughly. In other instances, it may be that you have a period of sustained focus and drive before "hitting a wall" and losing focus or energy. In either case, trying to continue working after you have left the "sweet spot" will result in spinning your wheels and losing efficiency.

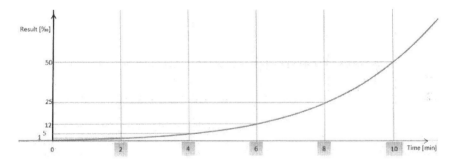

So, why is it the Ten-Minute Philosophy? I find that 10 minutes is a nice, easy number. It can even be two minutes and you will still see results if it is two minutes of sustained, daily action. With two minutes of course, the results will be smaller; the compounded effect will take about 50 times longer to materialize than with 10 minutes of daily work.

Every sustained action, no matter how small, will bring results.

This truth is the core of my philosophy. This approach will always triumph over the two major obstacles of any lasting change: fear of failure and giving up. Fear of failure stops you before you begin; giving up stops you some time later, but usually happens before the compounding results have become visible.

Every action brings results in the end. As long as you apply sustained energy to something, you can't fail. You have nothing to fear. You **can** start working toward your goals without the burden of hesitations and doubts.

If you believe, if you **know** that every sustained action brings results, giving up is out of the question; any incentives for resignation disappear.

"All right," you say, "I get the theories, but how are they applicable to my life?" I concur, theorizing doesn't drive results; what led me to embrace this philosophy wasn't stories or the preaching of others. It was my own experience.

In order to feel, at a gut level, that this is indeed a universal law that is applicable to you, I ask you to do a quick exercise. Take a moment to think of any successful area of your life. It can be anything - your marriage, a specific skill, a career, the fact you have never had a car accident, good grades at school, your great relationship with your parents. The best example for this exercise will be something that you take for granted, but that other people praise you for. So, pick one and think: what makes me successful in this area? What's the difference between me and the people who praise me for this? Chances are, they are less successful at it. What do I do that they don't?

I bet you will find some sustained action underlying your success.

I took for granted the love in my family. I hadn't noticed that it was anything special until my newfound online friends drew my attention to it through their comments on my personal blog. I gave it some thought and saw the sustained action. I tell my wife and kids I love them every day and I regularly make time to be with them. And this is just one instance of this law. I have found many other examples behind my big and small successes - my high-school diploma, the scholarship I received for my 4th year of university studies, my personal fitness progress.

If you look, you find examples of how this has already manifested in your own life. Embrace this philosophy and you will see the way it changes your daily actions and the way you manage your time.

It's no coincidence I decided to call this series "How to Change Your Life in 10 minutes a Day." In each book, I share at least one basic technique which takes 10 minutes a day or less and drives the biggest changes in each specific area. These techniques are successful, even for the busiest employee, parent, or entrepreneur.

We will begin exploring time management specifically in Chapter 4, but to do so without first discussing motivation would be to miss a key ingredient.

Action Items

- Make a list of things in your life you consider to be victories.
- For each victory, make a list of the sustained actions they took to achieve.
- Look for where the 'Ten Minute' philosophy has already worked for you and embrace it!

3

Motivation

"Until you value yourself, you won't value your time. Until you value your time, you will not do anything with it."

- M. Scott Peck

If you can answer at any given time, to any given person, without hesitation, the question, "What's your purpose in life?" you can go ahead and skip this chapter. If not, I urge you to read it closely. Your purpose must be the driving force behind improving your time management. Without a reason to do so, working on your time-management skills will not bring meaningful results.

Tips and techniques are great tools to have, but all the knowledge in the world will do you no good if you won't implement it. You need a purpose to do anything in life, managing your time included. That reason must be big enough to overcome the inertia, bigger than the multitude of reasons to take a break, to let go.

The time management process starts in your head. Your mind is the only true source of your procrastination. But, it's also the only true source of your productivity. The cynic or hardcore realist might find it hard to believe, but it is **the truth**. Nothing exists without first being created, and in your life, that **creation begins in your mind**.

Here is how the motivation story played out for me: I read *Getting Things Done* by David Allen in November 2011. Allen's book contains the most brilliant time management system I have ever seen. Everything is explained very clearly and arranged methodically. The system's simplicity and reported effectiveness led me to try it.

So, I tried and tried and tried ...

Trying was all I could achieve without the internal motivation. Don't get me wrong, every tip and technique, if used correctly, is fruitful. Even just **trying** Mr. Allen's methods **haphazardly** helped me manage my time better. But, by developing the motivation to **stand firmly behind** each technique, I began to see results that were greater by orders of magnitude!

Just think of someone doing his job because he is truly passionate about that work. Perhaps you have a coworker or friend who has that zeal for their work. Then think of someone who works just to get by. They may even do all of the same actions, after all it is the same job. But, the results they achieve and the amount of effort they both put in to achieve those results, are very different. Find just two examples from your experience and contemplate the differences.

In August 2012, I read another book that enabled me to manage my time even better than *Getting Things Done*. It wasn't a time management book at all; it was a personal development book titled *The Slight Edge* by Jeff Olson. This book drove me to seek meaningful change in my life. The self-improvement I worked on as a result, led to the development of an **impassioned motivation,** different from anything I had ever felt before. This new vigor gave me the ability to extract **far more value** from my time than ever before.

That's why I encourage you to search for your reasons first and, only then, apply these new time management techniques.

Why do you want to save time? Why do you want to be more effective? Why do you want to improve your productivity? What is the purpose behind those desires?

Forget wishes – they won't sustain you long enough to implement the techniques and build a new lifestyle.

Find your purpose

Stephen R. Covey became a household name and multi-millionaire through the pursuit of his passion for helping others grow. He began his greatest work - *The 7 Habits of Highly Effective People*, the bible of effectiveness - with a search for self-awareness and personal values. The secret is more spiritual than technical, isn't it?

I complied with his advice and doing so enhanced my effectiveness significantly. One of the first steps I took in transforming my life was to formulate my **personal mission statement**. It took me over a month of writing and rewriting, but it was worth every second. I advise you to do the very same thing.

Think of it as your greatest investment in your time management program, quite possibly your life. Your personal mission statement is THE key to improving your time management a thousand-fold. Why waste your time on minor tasks when you can invest a few weeks to skyrocket your awareness and motivation?

Lasting change must start from the level of principles and values. With this approach, you can do the (seemingly) impossible. This is how I've developed lasting and productive habits.

As of right now (October 2013), I track 33 habits on Lift. A year ago, I tracked just two. And I have a few more which have become so automatic that I don't need to track them anymore. Additionally, I have a few weekly and monthly habits that are also new. Overall, I've developed about 40 new habits in the last year.

Now, to the point: In 10 minutes on Google, I found countless links to pages with advice on creating or changing habits. All of them are compatible: start easy, start slowly; don't try to revolutionize your life.

http://www.self-improvement-mentor.com: "Changing a habit is one of the most difficult tasks that a person can undertake."

PsyBlog: "The classic mistake people make (...) is to bite off more than they can chew."

Leo Babauta: "(...) too many changes at once. I've seen that fail many times. (...) One habit change at a time. Some people can do two (...) and actually stick to it, but that's much more difficult. Once you get good at that, maybe you can do two at a time."

By "at a time," Mr. Babauta means 4-6 weeks of implementation. If diligent, it is possible to create 13 new, lasting habits in one year.

I didn't know that advice going in, so I did it my way and implemented over three times as many habits. And I got rid of several that consumed far too much time, like playing computer games or watching TV.

In case you didn't notice, 24 hours do not seem like enough to do all of my daily habits and have a life. But I still manage to do it, something I attribute solely to the power contained in my personal mission statement, my internal drive.

There are three elements of behavioral change in BJ Fogg's Behavior Model: Motivation, Ability and Trigger. According to the model, motivation and ability are interchangeable. So, if you have low motivation but high ability, you can still succeed with your change. And vice versa - if you don't know how to introduce a change, but your motivation is high, you will find a way to succeed.

Finally, I had found something to explain my success: I have enormously high motivation (found through developing my mission statement). My abilities probably pale in comparison to the abilities of many people out there, and yet I have become more effective and successful than ever before!

If you don't buy the 'feelings approach,' then refer to the science. Do you want to manage your time efficiently, but don't know how? Then your Ability factor, in this area, is low and you need ... that's right, a high motivation. Again, this is where a personal mission statement can clarify what things drive you and help you to develop a new sense of motivation.

Define your life's purpose and your path to success will become evident. I've done many different things, for many different reasons, but I found there is no motivation like that which came with the realization of my life's purpose.

If you haven't already, I strongly recommend that you read the first two chapters of *The 7 Habits of Highly Effective People* and write your personal mission statement. If you want to save some money, you can buy my book "A Personal Mission Statement: Your Roadmap to Happiness" for $1[1] and learn how to compose one. Or, if you have a lot of time for research, you can figure out it on your own; browse the Web and you will find volumes of advice about the process.

The action-oriented may see this step as a waste of time, but I assure you that action without contemplation is the true waste of time. Why? Because only sustained action brings lasting results. Without a purpose, sooner or later you will give up, even if you are – like me – extremely stubborn.

An example: I have been doing push-ups every day for half my life. Before I found a good enough reason, I started and abandoned this habit more times than I like to count. It took me about a decade to figure it out. My stubbornness was enough to keep me going for a

---

[1] On the US market. On other markets additional fees or taxes may be applied.

year or two at a time, but it's the internal sense of purpose that has kept me going consistently for the last six years.

Your mindset is the foundation of your 'personal house.' Walls and a roof without a foundation is no more than a tent, and a tent probably won't withstand heavy rain or high winds.

Action Items

- **Create your own personal mission statement or use any alternative method which will help you to answer the question, "What is your purpose in life?"**
- **If you are an action-oriented, down-to-earth type of person, study BJ Fogg's Behavior Model first.**

4

The Ultimate Time Management Tool

"The bad news is time flies. The good news is you're the pilot."

— Michael Altshuler

As I pointed out in the previous chapter, time management starts in your head. You need to work on your mindset to see any significant results.

Don't worry, I won't force you to murmur the mantra: "I will do everything the most efficient way every minute, every day ..." ten times a day. I believe affirmation can be a top-shelf tool for achieving results. I also believe, though, that it is a tool that requires mastery to produce significant results. Anyone can repeat mantras, but getting real life results from doing this is an art I certainly haven't mastered.

The tool I'm talking about is much simpler. You need just two skills to use it; skills you have had since childhood. All that this tool requires is that you are able to write and tell the time.

The ultimate tool I am referring to is the **time journal.** The time journal works so amazingly well because of **its effectiveness and its simplicity**. Anybody can use it.

You may be thinking, "Oh, gimme a break; I know all about the time journal!" I'll deal with this attitude a little further on. But if the idea is new to you, pay attention. A time journal is just a journal in which you write all your activities and how much time they take. The more specific you are about the kind of activity you've done and about the amount of time it took, the better it will work.

The minimum recommended by Jim Rohn is at least one entry in the time journal every 30 minutes. You can note time spans or mark the beginning and end of activities. Some schools of thought also suggest that you write down your moods and distractions. Choose the method most suitable for you. If you carry a smartphone, there are plenty of time tracking apps can help you. Or you can simply use a pen and paper. Just pick your golden rule, whatever is most convenient for you and stick with it.

I decided to start keeping a time journal, so I wrote down every activity I found myself doing and marked the start and stop times. I spend half of my life in front of a computer, so I used Excel to keep all of these entries. If I was away from the computer, I would jot things down in a pocket notepad and enter them in my spreadsheet as soon as I returned to the computer.

To get a picture of what I'm talking about, take a peek into the beginning of my day on July 4, 2013:

1	begin time	end time	Activity	time span
2	22:05	4:55	sleep	6:50
3	4:55	5:03	bathroom, drink water, medicate nose	0:08
4	5:03	5:17	workout, listen to audio materials	0:14
5	5:17	5:23	brush teeth, listen to audio materials	0:06
6	5:23	5:32	prepare for work	0:09
7	5:32	5:37	excercise - dips	0:05
8	5:37	5:41	prepare for work	0:04
9	5:41	5:48	walk to train, prayer	0:07
10	5:48	5:51	read my philosophy notes	0:03
11	5:51	5:57	self-analysis exercise	0:06
12	5:57	6:01	time tracking	0:04
13	6:01	6:52	write 550 words	0:51
14	6:52	6:58	walk to bus, listen to my personal mission statement	0:06
15	6:58	7:25	bus ride, speed reading exercise	0:27
16	7:25	7:30	walk to the office, listen to my personal mission statement	0:05
17	7:30	7:34	prepare for work and time tracking	0:04
18	7:34	7:41	work related tasks	0:07
19	7:41	8:03	self-analysis exercise	0:22
20	8:03	8:33	write	0:30
21	8:33	8:40	breakfast - had watermelon	0:07

You don't have to write down every detail. Again, for this to become **a sustained habit**, you need to do it in a way that **works for you**.

I used abbreviations for common activities to make the process faster. What you see above is the version translated to common language, to make it understandable. The start time of an activity is taken automatically from the end time of the previous activity by an Excel formula. Another formula calculates the activity's time span. It saved me time over inputting this manually.

See the "time tracking" entries? Those are the points when I turned on the computer on a train and at the office (5:57 and 7:30 respectively) and rewrote the entries from my pocket notepad into an Excel sheet. After 7:34, I hardly needed any time dedicated solely to time tracking, as it was just a matter of changing the window on the computer, marking the time and jotting down an activity name.

Feel free to download and use my template: www.onedollartips.com/tools/time_journal_templa te

Remember to manually input sleep time in the first cell!

There are people, like successful serial entrepreneur Rich Schefren of Strategic Profits, who ingrain their version of the time journal into their everyday activities and it becomes second nature for them. I recommend strict use of a detailed version (as presented in the fragment of my journal) for just two weeks. Repeat this exercise every few months to keep your level of awareness high.

If you have any reservations about keeping a time journal, think it over. Yes, it can be a little pesky to exercise such control over your day. Yes, it's a little strange to do and can make you feel like a weirdo, but are there really any other disadvantages to paying such close attention to where your time goes? None come to mind for me and I promise you **the advantages are much greater**.

This is your first step in building a more productive mindset. By keeping a time journal, you make yourself **aware** of how you spend your time. If you are interested in implementing a new time management strategy, it's likely because you don't use your time optimally. The time journal allows you to get to the **core of the problem**, to very clearly see areas where you are wasting time.

That's the main purpose of using this tool - to make you aware of how you really use your time. You can't improve if you don't know your starting position. **Most people believe they already know precisely how they use their time. Most people are wrong.**

There are dangers you should be aware of that come with keeping a time journal. By being conscious about tracking your time, you may find yourself changing your behavior just to make a more impressive journal. For a couple of weeks, you might limit your unproductive activities and then, as soon as you finish the tracking exercise, slip back into old, less effective habits.

Modern technology gives us tools that can help. If you spend a lot of time on the computer and using mobile devices, I recommend the RescueTime application. It runs in the background, gathering information about how you are spending your time. You can install it, forget about it and check back a week, or a month later.

Knowledge, awareness and progress tracking are keys to making any improvement. If you rush blindly into a venture just hoping everything will be all right, you are asking for trouble. If you do not first recognize where you are starting from, and don't measure your progress, you are setting yourself up to fail.

Be serious about keeping your time journal. If you have never successfully done this, have never tried, or tried and gave up, this is a must-do. Don't preoccupy yourself with what method you use to track your time – that's not the point. The point is that, whatever system you implement, you will become very aware of your baseline productivity and will see it improve before your eyes.

Drop the excuses and do it! It simple, it's easy, it works. The big shots - Darren Hardy, Jim Rohn, Rich Schefren - have all used this technique and they all recommend it as a powerful productivity tool.

Action Items

- **Choose the most suitable form of recording your time journal.**
- **Keep a detailed time journal for two weeks.**
- **Use RescueTime for two weeks after this and check to see if you have slipped into any old habits.**
- **Use the time journal for two weeks every quarter.**

5

Work on What's Important, Not What's Urgent

"Most of us spend too much time on what is urgent and not enough time on what is important."

— Stephen R. Covey

If you've studied time management in any depth, you probably know the important/urgent activity matrix. If not, then check out this witty summary.

You must work on important projects to be effective. Again, it's a matter of your priorities. If you don't know the source of your motivation, you will tend to drift in the direction of other people's agendas. You will spend your time working on 'emergencies,' instead of on what's really important to you.

You may be very efficient in dealing with urgent issues, but still not be effective in the end - the proverbial "spinning your wheels." It may be appreciated at your job; it even may be crucial to your career (for example, if you are a doctor in emergency services). But it's highly unlikely to create the life of your dreams in the long run. Even a fireman's job doesn't consist solely of emergencies. There are long hours of training and supplementary education, new devices to learn, new recruits to train. Managing only the urgent issues is not enough.

That's why it's crucial to know your goal, to know your purpose, before you even start to make plans.

In an ideal world, you would spend 100% of your time on Quadrant 2 activities. Our world is not ideal, however, so I would suggest adhering as closely as possible to the 80/20 rule and trying to spend 80% of your time on the most important 20% of your tasks - the Quadrant 2 activities.

Let's see a real life example to explain the idea clearly.

I have a lot of urgent matters to take care of in my life. I have to pay bills. I have to be on time to the office. I have to solve immediate problems in my employer's database infrastructure. I have to buy groceries or prepared meals. But all of these activities are not that important to my true purpose. I could outsource most of them, if I had the resources. Often I find I have the choice to organize these things differently, as well (I can telecommute and do my job from home as efficiently as in the office).

A big part of my purpose is to be a writer. It's important to me, yet it's absolutely non-urgent. If I don't write, no disasters will occur. I will still be able to do my 9 to 5 job, to pay bills and buy groceries. I just won't get closer to fulfilling my purpose.

And that's why I make writing my top priority. I have over 40 daily habits, but writing is the most critical one. Every working day, I commit to writing at least 400 words and a minimum of 30 minutes.

Is it 11 p.m. and I still haven't written today? Even if I'm getting up for work the next day at 4:30 a.m., I stay awake and write until I achieve both of those metrics. Every day. Am I a superhuman? No, I do it because **I know my priorities.**

Action Items

- **Familiarize yourself with the important/urgent activity matrix.**
- **List all your regular activities and your goals and match them to a quadrant in the matrix.**

6

Don't Kill Your Time

"Lost time is never found again."
— Benjamin Franklin

One harsh reality the time journal will expose is the ways in which you waste time - your time killers. Every person has them. Mine were watching TV and playing computer games, reading popular novels, surfing Internet news and commenting on news articles just for the sake of commenting. I spent hours on those activities every day.

Do whatever it takes to convince yourself that time killers are keeping you from your life's purpose. Sitting in front of the computer or TV for hours **rarely** provides any **lasting value** to your life. This is time you could utilize in the pursuit of your personal mission.

One of the common regrets of people on their deathbed[2] is, "I wish I didn't work so hard." Another is, "I wish that I had let myself be happier." But this doesn't mean people want to just hang out, wasting their time on meaningless or trivial matters. Is watching that sitcom making you happy? No, it just makes you feel good for the moment. It's a transient anesthetic.

Two out of the five most common regrets of dying people regard courage and busting out of your comfort zone. How much courage do you need to put your butt on the couch and turn on the TV?

The last common regret is: "I wish I had stayed in touch with my friends." Notice it's not, "I wish I had played more Call of Duty with my friends," or "I wish I had watched more movies with my friends." Those activities are vehicles to spend time with your friends, not the goals themselves.

Analyze how you spend your time. Pin down the time killers you use to feel better; activities which don't bring you closer to your purpose, but take up much of your time. Cut them ruthlessly from your life. As long as your yardstick is your purpose, it's relatively easy to root out these worthless activities. Just replace them with something worth doing, something truly fulfilling.

Killing time is suicide in installments. I cannot word it any stronger. If you are not actively living, actively growing, you are dying.

I no longer play computer games. I've read only two fiction books since October 2012. I severely limited my

---

[2] http://www.inspirationandchai.com/Regrets-of-the-Dying.html

time spent wandering around the Internet and watching TV. These activities are simply not attractive to me anymore. I prefer writing, studying and spending quality time with my family instead.

Action Items

- **Make a list of your leisure activities.**
- **Measure the usefulness of each activity against the yardstick of your purpose. Next to those that advance your purpose, write how they contribute. Next to those that do not, write ELIMINATE.**

7

Work Every Day

"I think and think for months and years. Ninety-nine times, the conclusion is false. The hundredth time I am right."

— Albert Einstein

There is magic in consistency. I don't know the science behind it, but it's true. Getting back on track after holidays or sick leave is a struggle. Every Monday is a struggle, isn't it? Observe the mood at your office the next time you start a new work week.

Consistency is key, so work on your important projects as often as you can, preferably every day. Consistency builds **momentum and continuity,** while destroying inertia. It doesn't have to be a grand action each day. Do something small, but do it regularly.

I used to write only on workdays and take a break from writing on weekends. Getting back to the writing routine was always hard on Mondays. So I began writing every day, and in three weeks had been far more productive than my most productive month prior.

I set a guideline for myself to write at least 400 words each weekend. I overcame my obstacles. Busy Saturday? I just get up half an hour earlier.

I have a "no work on Sunday" rule. So on Sundays, my efforts are spent working on my novel or my personal blog - activities that are for my enjoyment, not for work.

Weekend writing has led to an additional 15,000 words in 2013 and will accumulate into 40,000 more in 2014.

On workdays, I set an 800-word minimum, but I achieved an average of over 1,000 words per day during those 3 weeks - at least a 25% increase in productivity!

Action Items

- **Plan a daily discipline which will bring you closer to realizing your purpose; it doesn't have to be lofty, it just has to be consistent**
- **Practice it every day. Keep track of the time spent in your time journal.**

8

Break it Down

"Very easy to understand; very straightforward. But these are powerful and effective productivity techniques"

— Jim Rohn

The biggest threat to your productivity is your psychology. We are odd creatures. We are scared of our dreams, especially the big ones. When you look at an enormous task in front of you - writing a book, launching a website, establishing a business, preparing your kids to be effective, successful adults - it is easy to be immediately discouraged. It seems like so much work! How can one single man or woman accomplish it all?

In the case of tasks you have no choice about, like raising a child, you just somehow manage to achieve them. If you are like most people, you give up on tasks you "know" are just too big. You use excuses and procrastinate. The world will not end if you don't publish your book in this decade, will it? So you postpone it for an unspecified future.

This is **mental trickery**. You are just as capable of starting a business or writing a book as you are of raising a kid. You will need a different mental trick to overcome this fear - breaking huge tasks into a series of tiny ones.

Break the task down to the point where you will feel ridiculous if you avoid such a minor effort. If writing a book within two years feels like a challenge, then maybe writing one chapter a month is more reasonable? Does it still look too big? Break it down further, decide to write 10 pages a week. Can you do it? If you think back to writing essays in high school and you feel it still surpasses your capability, break it down further: A page a day? A paragraph per writing session? A single sentence every hour?

Can you write one sentence each hour? Sure you can. It's easy.

You have now out-tricked the mental trickery. It went from, "I can't write a book," to "It's easy to write a book."

Writing a book is a comfortable example. It's easy to imagine how to divide the writing process into smaller chunks. More complex tasks can be more problematic.

This brings us to another tip for breaking down tasks: write it down.

Let's take launching a new website, for example. Launching a website requires many tasks: domain name, hosting, specific technologies, design, graphics, multimedia, content, marketing, SEO ... Seems overwhelming, doesn't it? This is the mental trickery taking hold. Take it out of your head and write it down. Marshall the points into chronological order. Take the first point and break it down into even smaller chunks (you must actually write it down). If you prefer to do this on a computer, trello.com offers a great project management tool that is free and easy to use.

Example:

Domain name - what is required? Write it out:

- brainstorm ideas for the website's name
- research the availability of the best five
- comparison shop 5 domain providers
- buy domain from the best provider

Everything now appears simpler, more doable. Your mind is no longer occupied by appalling visions of a monstrous task; it focuses on small and manageable details.

As long as you keep your **vague and imprecise plans** in your head, your mind can play with them and make **bogeymen** out of them. **Write them down** and your ability to perform them will **increase tenfold.**

Writing down all the subtasks allows you to prioritize and serialize them, deciding what to do first, what to do next and so on. It also reveals the interdependencies between subtasks (e.g. choosing a specific technology may limit your hosting choices). All those steps will help you make better use of your time, but it's very hard to manage them all in your head. That's why they must be written down.

Action Items

- Write down all your projects (or create a trello board for them).
- Break down bigger tasks into smaller chunks and repeat the process until each task is broken into its smallest subtasks.
- Prioritize and serialize the subtasks, taking note of interdependencies and tasks that have a specific order.

9

Use a To Do List

"Rename your "To-Do" list to your "Opportunities" list. Each day is a treasure chest filled with limitless opportunities; take joy in checking many off your list."

— Steve Maraboli

The dictionary definition of a to-do list is: a list of tasks that need to be completed, typically organized in order of priority.

The to-do list is the foundation of every time management system I've ever encountered. To organize your time, you need first to know what to do. Different systems offer different variations on this theme: daily, weekly, monthly, priority, job related, home related ...

Your job is to work out which will be most effective for you.

I was initially attracted to the precise system of neatly organized groups as recommended in David Allen's *Getting Things Done* system. Unfortunately, it doesn't work very well for me; I have no central place to gather all the day-to-day obligations, what Allen calls the "inbox." I have labeled alarms on my company phone, company mailbox and private mailbox, as well as my notepad with ideas and projects, a spreadsheet with deadlines and two different software programs at work with ongoing tasks to take care of. It's hard to connect data from so many different input systems into one master list. It's doable, but managing this central system means additional work, which is not worth it.

Another possibility is to prepare your to-do list first thing in the morning, or for the next day before going to sleep. This also doesn't work for me. I'm unable to plan my day beforehand because it always seems as though some interruption comes up.

At first, this discouraged me. I tried several times to plan my day ahead of time. Then something would go astray and leave me feeling that I had wasted the time spent on planning the day before.

But even with my hectic schedule, I still use to-do lists. Again, keeping everything in your head is a losing proposition. My system is tailored to my life and may or may not work for you. Think about your daily schedule and habits and decide how to best use a to-do list in your life. Then, actually use it!

Now I basically use two lists. The first is my daily habits list, which comprises about 30 habits. I've broken down some of the most important projects into daily chunks - working on my websites and blogs, networking through social media, reading, studying, writing. I prioritize them; some are more important than others. For example, I can skip my workout or reading a blog post on my mentor's site if absolutely necessary, but I have to write and study the Bible every day.

I arrange the habit list, more or less, in the order of my day. My morning ritual habits - reading fragments of three different works, reviewing my vision board, repeating my personal mission statement and so on - are at the beginning. My "online" habits - visiting my friends' sites, following my mentors, working on my website and a few others - are in the middle. And in the evening, I work on habits like my gratitude diaries. I go through the list many times each day and check off the completed items. I began using Lift to keep track of these habits at the end of September 2013, but before that I just used a paper notepad.

The other list I use is a simple set of items to be done that I keep in my pocket notepad. I always carry this notepad with me. This list contains the items which I don't do regularly, like ordering a book cover on Fiverr.com or paying the electricity bill. As soon as I do an item, I cross it out. I don't prioritize or arrange the points on this list much. Some items are minor; some are major – but the importance of a task is clear as soon as I look at the list. I don't need any special ordering system to realize that buying my wife a gift for our wedding anniversary is more important than writing feedback for the software I decided to return a month ago.

I purge and rewrite this list about once a month, or whenever all the crossed-out points get too messy.

That's it, no rocket science. I will probably modify this system when I become self-employed, but for now, it serves me well.

Lay down your own system in a similar fashion, but don't copy someone else's approach verbatim. Read, study, borrow some hints and compose your own custom-made system. Just keep in mind that the most important factor is how you will implement it in your life. It may take some time to tweak it into a system that works with your life, but don't give up! A to-do list system that is truly compatible with your life is magic!

Action Items

- **Write down all of your typical tasks; cover all the areas of your life - your job, family obligations, obligations with your church or other organizations you belong to, even your hobbies.**
- **Try different arrangements of those tasks to make a single list or a few of them; organize them by priority, where you need to do them, when you need to do them. Experiment until you find your ideal configuration.**

10

Block Your Time

"Realize that now, in this moment of time, you are creating. You are creating your next moment. That is what's real."

— Sara Paddison

What does it mean to block your time? Blocking time is dedicating a specific period of time for a specific task. Guess where all this starts? Yep, it starts in your head! We are back to the motivation factor again.

I've heard a lot of sound advice on this topic. Wake up earlier and do the job, find your "magic time" (when you are most productive) and reserve that for important tasks, use the Pomodoro technique, avoid distractions, check your email just twice a day. The list goes on and on.

My past choices have made me a slave to the agendas of others. I work as a database administrator, a job very similar to that of a fireman. Usually, I wait patiently for a disaster and when one comes along, I drop everything else at that moment and extinguish the fire (save the data). Often, this gives me long periods of time to do with what I please, but sometimes I honestly don't have five minutes to spare.

What about waking up early? I work on a shift system. I live over 30 miles from my office. To get to work by 7, I need to wake up at 4:25 a.m. Well, I could go to sleep earlier and wake up even earlier, right? No, I have a wife and kids, and am dedicated to spending quality time with them. This makes it impossible for me to go to sleep before 9 p.m.

The shift system and family are very good at seizing my "magic time."

As for distractions, I need to have my work mailbox open at all times to respond to incoming alarms. The same goes for my Internet browser; several times a day, I need to use Google for work-related research.

But none of the factors above give me an excuse to not manage my time. I view them simply as realities that must be accounted for in my time management system.

I used to wake up 4:55 a.m. on weekdays, but now I get up 30 minutes earlier and use this time to ignite my day. I review my personal mission statement and vision board. I read fragments of two books which have shaped my philosophy. I read fragments of the philosophy manifesto I composed for myself. I sit at my kitchen table for 10 to 20 minutes to reflect on my life and state of mind. I write down these ruminations.

I decided that this is the best use of this 30 minutes. Those are the only ironclad minutes of focus, peace and quiet in my day.

I consciously check my Facebook account and private inbox only 2-3 times per day. I usually do it as a reward for completing other tasks, or as a way to relax for a few minutes. The same goes with reading news. I also force myself to check my sales on Amazon no more than once a day.

I try to block my time for writing. It is the first thing I want to tackle every day. It takes quite a lot of time – anywhere from 40 minutes to two hours each day. I love to write on the train during my commute to and from work. I put earphones in and just concentrate on writing. On the train, there are no emails, no alarms, no people needing my attention. I said "I try to block my time" because the journey to work takes me about 60 minutes, so if I write longer than that, I'm forced to do it at work or at home. These are environments that tend to strain my focus.

Blocking your time also means is that you dedicate that time for only one specific purpose. So when I write, I write. When someone interrupts me - a coworker asking for help; my kids asking for dinner - I deal with the issue and then go back to writing. I don't try to juggle multiple tasks at a time. I do one task as long as necessary to finish the job for that day, then I go on to the next task in my queue.

There are many ideas on how to block your time, but they all come down to making you concentrate on one task at a time. One of the stranger bits of advice I've heard comes from entrepreneur Pat Flynn. He advises doing the dishes to put yourself into a work mindset. It is work, but it goes by quickly and is pretty mindless, meaning you can begin to mentally prepare for your next task. Sound silly? Perhaps, but then again, Pat Flynn earns more than $500k a year. It doesn't cost anything to try this method, and maybe it will work for you, too. The idea is to research different techniques and try them for yourself, then stick with the solution most suitable for your unique situation.

All of the above advice has one thing in common: to do something, you need to give the work at hand your unwavering attention. **You have control over your attention.** Use it!

Action Items

- **Prioritize your to-do lists and block time for each task.**
- **Review and try the techniques mentioned in this chapter and pick the one that works best for you.**

11

Eat that Frog

"Eat a live frog first thing in the morning and nothing worse will happen to you the rest of the day."

— Mark Twain

Do you know why I deal with writing as soon as possible? Because it's daunting. Especially if I'm trying to meet a deadline. I admire reporters who produce article after article, day after day. If I'm excited about the subject, I write effortlessly. But I'm not always lucky enough to be writing about something that truly excites me.

So whatever task intimidates you most – do it first. Then, "nothing worse will happen." Every other job will be a cinch, in comparison. Completing the tough task first will give you a boost of productivity. You will feel like a winner, an achiever, and that will give you more energy to work on the next projects.

This tip drives to the core of human behavior. By **facing the hardest job first**, you are **building your**

willpower, day by day. After only a short while, you will be invincible.

Many successful people teach that success comes from venturing out of your comfort zone. In *The 4-Hour Workweek*, Tim Ferris gives the reader a challenge to simply lay down in the middle of a crowded public place for 10 seconds. The aim of that exercise is to get comfortable with the uncomfortable.

Train yourself in the habit of success. **Overcoming obstacles, excuses and fears is always a victory.** Facing the 'hard' task is really about overcoming fear, isn't it?

I try to organize my activities in order of difficulty. After a daily portion of writing, I go ahead with my "online" habits - I participate in online communities; I work on my website; I read my mentors' blogs; I comment. I don't like the mundane tasks on my websites - adding categories, editing the pages, including links, managing comments, installing plug-ins and so on. I find them boring, so I get them out of the way early. I love to read, so I leave the reading for the end of the day.

Don't stop with the first tough job. If you have a choice, pick another difficult, stressful or boring task from the list and conquer it next. Start your day strong and you will be more productive overall. You will feel better about yourself, which will bear fruits tomorrow, when you will face new challenges.

Action Items

- Make a habit of taking on the hardest task first each day.
- Exercise stepping out of your comfort zone.

12

The Sand Grains Method

"Who makes quick use of the moment is a genius of prudence."

— Johann Kaspar Lavater

I developed this name for one of my fundamental time management strategies. Using the Sand Grains Method, you fill your minutes with tiny tasks, the "grains of sand."

This approach is one of the core ideas in David Allen's *Getting Things Done* system. You put every single task on your list and then manage your time based on them. If you have a five-minute walk from the bus to the office, use that time to call a friend you've been meaning to call. If you are tired and need a break between job-related tasks, instead of surfing the Internet mindlessly, pick a task from your 'to do on the Internet' list: searching for a specific book on Amazon or reading that blog post you bookmarked a week ago.

Just as you can more efficiently fill a jar with sand than with stones, the sand grains method allows you to

increase your "productivity density." I structure my habits around this idea. As I mentioned in Chapter 2, I have many activities which take 10 minutes or less. Speed reading practice, studying the Bible, doing pull-ups, reviewing my vision board, a High-Intensity Interval Training workout and adding my website to a web catalog all require 10 minutes at most.

It's really easy to fit several 10-minute blocks of time into your daily schedule. And that's exactly what I do.

The Sand Grains Method also helps in avoiding boredom and monotony. I jump from one task to another, and I feel the joy of achievement each time I cross out even a tiny activity from my daily plan. When my focus is strained from working on a long or complex task, I often feel the temptation to distract myself. I'm sure you are familiar with that urge to open Facebook or browse a news website. In such cases, I take one of the small tasks from my to-do list and complete it. This small accomplishment energizes me for further work on the bigger task.

Of course, not every type of activity is suitable for 10-minute blocks. I've been forced before to write in 10-minute installments, but I am much more productive if I write for 60-120 minutes at a time.

We are talking about fillers here, not your core activities. Believe it or not, even physical exercise can be a 'sand grain' activity. I don't plan long sessions on a treadmill or jogging outside. I just do a series of push-ups or other similar exercises here and there, a few times a day. For a white collar worker, it's enough to stay in shape.

Develop a plan for how to fill your schedule. Chop bigger tasks into smaller chunks and do them "in the meantime." If your job is to contact 100 people this month, divide it as described in chapter 7 and send 3-4 emails a day. Composing and sending a single message, especially if using a template, takes mere minutes; you can fit it in whenever you wish.

Each time you do a tiny job, you feel satisfaction from completing a task and it fuels your energy.

Always have something to do. I commute up to four hours every workday, and I see how people waste their time on buses and trains. I don't remember the last time I stared idly out of a train window. There are endless possibilities for filling that time! You can read, study, write, listen to a podcast, or do any combination thereof. Just be creative.

Action Items

- **Prepare a list of fillers in advance; don't spend your energy on wondering what to do next when you have a few minutes to spare.**
- **Break big tasks into smaller chunks, so you can do them "in the meantime."**

13

Multi-Tasking

"There's never enough time to do all the nothing you want."

— Bill Watterson

Multi-tasking gets a lot of bad press in the time management world. The common suggestion is to avoid it whenever possible. And rightfully so! I shudder each time I see my son doing homework and watching TV at the same time.

But...

You can do at least two things at once when one task is fairly mindless. Driving a car, doing the dishes, putting away laundry, cooking, cleaning - you do most of these jobs without straining your brain too much, don't you? What's more, you spend a lot of time on them. When I track all of my daily activities, I discover that I spend over two hours each day on such mundane tasks.

So use your mind while you are doing a purely physical job. Let me show you several examples from my own experience.

I listen to podcasts and audiobooks during my morning workout and while brushing my teeth.

I pray each time I walk to and from the train station or bus stop, and while doing household chores.

I've fallen in love with my Saturday multi-tasking. I listen to long hours of educational and motivational materials while vacuuming or scrubbing the toilet. I listen to them while running errands.

While getting to sleep and waking up, I pray and/or repeat my personal mission statement in my mind. It is soothing – I sleep like a baby and I start my day full of energy and enthusiasm, even though that day starts at 4:25 a.m.

It's your turn. What can you do mentally while in the cafeteria queue? While driving? While swimming or sitting in the sauna? During your commute or in the dentist's waiting room?

Here are some ideas:

- **Prayer:** I read a lot of books written by saints, and they overwhelmingly agree that prayer and work are not exclusive. Most of them insist that prayer boosts one's earthly productivity.
- **Visualization:** To plan for success, you need a vision of a better tomorrow. You don't need special meditation sessions in a peaceful environment; using your imagination requires only your mind.

- **Planning:** This is similar to visualization; however, to plan something even as simple as a grocery list, it's very handy to have a pen and notepad at your disposal.
- **Repeating affirmations or your mission statement:** Here's another activity that only uses your mind. I'm skeptical of using too many affirmations. It's very hard for me to connect the dots, to find a relationship between something I say in my mind and a tangible result. Having said that, I have one or two that I repeat every day because they work for me. Another daily activity is repeating my 1,300-word personal mission statement.
- **Self-analysis:** Just converse with yourself, have a set of uncomfortable questions for yourself. I do it every day, with pen in hand, writing the answers down. Nevertheless, it's better to ask yourself constructive questions, without writing down the answers, than to let your mind wander idly while you do the dishes.

The mind is huge and the above examples are just a few of the boundless possibilities for mental-physical multitasking. One year at university, I got a summer job in a factory. I had to stand at the production line hour after hour doing manual labor. While I did this, however, I was also writing computer programs in my head. Be creative.

Another advantage of all these mental activities is that you are exerting control over your mind. Most of us are often unaware of what's going on in our minds. I was unaware for much of my life. Self-talk was something I took for granted. I no longer really listened to myself, I simply reacted, like in an old marriage or old friendship. I was with myself for so long that I was convinced I knew everything there was to know about me.

Often, self-talk is B.S., a projection of our fears and believed limitations. Les Brown presents this vividly: each time he had an aspiration, his other self would come up with obstacles and excuses: "Who are you to achieve success? You don't even know your parents! You didn't go to college! You can't be a motivational speaker!" By taking active control of your mental energies, you begin to strip your mind of these automatic, defeatist thoughts.

Action Items

- **Write down a list of physical activities you can use for multi-tasking.**
- **Schedule 15 minutes for brainstorming what you can put your mind into while doing the physical activities.**
- **Match at least one physical and one mental activity, and start practicing mental-physical multi-tasking.**

Conclusion

"The time is always right to do what is right."
— Martin Luther King, Jr.

Now you know the basics, go and implement them. The techniques I have shared with you are not rocket science, but they do require **sustained effort**.

Start managing your time and never give up. I found I couldn't fully implement Dave Allen's *Getting Things Done* method, but just trying it gave me an incentive to seek strategies that better fit my life. I've been amazed by my progress and productivity. I've transformed from employee (slave) into a blogger and writer who expects to be self-employed one day. You never know what you will unleash until you start!

Persevere. Don't buy today's hype. Anything worthwhile takes time to develop. Don't expect to be managing a Fortune 500 company by next year.

Fine-tune your methods. I deliberately avoided giving you an easy formula to follow. You have to explore this jigsaw puzzle and put it together in a way that will work for **you**.

I strongly recommend starting with the time journal first, but make your own decision as needed. Just pick one of the techniques I shared and start practicing it **today**. Develop your own disciplines along the way.

I would appreciate you sending me an email with news about your progress. I want to celebrate with you in your victories. Give me a peek into your story by sending a message to: timemanagement@onedollartips.com or a tweet (@StawickiMichal).

Whatever your true purpose is – wherever your goals are pulling you – **I know that you have all the ability and the time needed to succeed on your path and beyond.** And I look forward to rejoicing with you when you experience success!

Free Gift for You

Thanks for reading all the way to the end. If you made it this far, you must have liked it!

I really appreciate having people all over the world take interest in the thoughts, ideas, research, and words that I share in my books. I appreciate it so much that I invite you to visit: www.michalzone.com, where you can register to receive all of my future releases absolutely free.

You won't receive any annoying emails or product offers or anything distasteful by being subscribed to my mailing list. This is purely an invite to receive my future book releases for free as a way of saying thanks to you for taking a sincere interest in my work.

Once again, that's www.michalzone.com

A Favor Please

I used to actively discourage my readers from giving me a review immediately after they read my book. I asked you for a review only once you began seeing results. This approach was against common sense and standard practice. Reviews are crucial for a book's visibility on Amazon. And my approach severely hindered me from getting my message out to people just like you, who stand to benefit from it.

I was convinced about that when "Master Your Time in 10 Minutes a Day" became a best-seller. Essentially, I've gotten a number of reviews in a short amount of time, but most of those reviews were the 'plastic' ones we all dislike on Amazon: "Great book! Great content! Great reading! Great entertainment!" Such reviews simply don't carry much weight; anybody could leave a review like that without even reading the book.

In the end, it didn't matter, and my book skyrocketed up the best-seller ranks, anyway. More people than ever have had the chance to get my book in their hands. I'm grateful for this, because more people have received the means to take control over their time and their destiny.

I want to ask a favor of you. If you have found value in this book, please take a moment and share your opinion with the world. Just let me know what you learned and how it affected you in a positive way. Your reviews help me to positively change the lives of others. Thank you!

About the Author

I'm Michal Stawicki and I live in Poland, Europe. I've been married for over 14 years and am the father of two boys and one girl. I work full time in the IT industry, and recently, I've become an author. My passions are transparency, integrity and progress.

In August 2012, I read a book called "The Slight Edge" by Jeff Olson. It took me a whole month to start implementing ideas from this book. That led me to reading numerous other books on personal development, some effective, some not so much. I took a look at myself and decided this was one person who could surely use some development.

In November of 2012, I created my personal mission statement; I consider it the real starting point of my progress. Over several months time, I applied several self-help concepts and started building inspiring results: I lost some weight, greatly increased my savings, built new skills and got rid of bad habits while developing better ones.

I'm very pragmatic, a "down to earth" person. I favor utilitarian, bottom-line results over pure artistry. Despite the ridiculous language, however, I found there is value in the "hokey-pokey visualization" stuff and I now see it as my mission to share what I have learned.

My books are not abstract. I avoid going mystical as much as possible. I don't believe that pure theory is what we need in order to change our lives; the Internet age has proven this quite clearly. What you will find in my books are:

- detailed techniques and methods describing how you can improve your skills and drive results in specific areas of your life
- real life examples
- personal stories

So, whether you are completely new to personal development or have been crazy about the Law of Attraction for years, if you are looking for concrete strategies, you will find them in my books. My writing shows that I am a relatable, ordinary guy and not some ivory tower guru.

Made in the USA
Middletown, DE
09 September 2017